© **Copyright 2021 - All rights reserved.**

You may not reproduce, duplicate or send the contents of this book without direct written permission from the author. You cannot hereby despite any circumstance blame the publisher or hold him or her to legal responsibility for any reparation, compensations, or monetary forfeiture owing to the information included herein, either in a direct or an indirect way.

Legal Notice: This book has copyright protection. You can use the book for personal purpose. You should not sell, use, alter, distribute, quote, take excerpts or paraphrase in part or whole the material contained in this book without obtaining the permission of the author first.

Disclaimer Notice: You must take note that the information in this document is for casual reading and entertainment purposes only. We have made every attempt to provide accurate, up to date and reliable information. We do not express or imply guarantees of any kind. The persons who read admit that the writer is not occupied in giving legal, financial, medical or other advice. We put this book content by sourcing various places.

Please consult a licensed professional before you try any techniques shown in this book. By going through this document, the book lover comes to an agreement that under no situation is the author accountable for any forfeiture, direct or indirect, which they may incur because of the use of material contained in this document, including, but not limited to, — errors, omissions, or inaccuracies.

HOW TO DRAW ANIMALS STEP BY STEP FOR KIDS

This book belongs to:

Steven Cottontail Manor

HOW TO DRAW SQUIRREL

Redraw the previous animal

HOW TO DRAW SNAIL

Redraw the previous animal

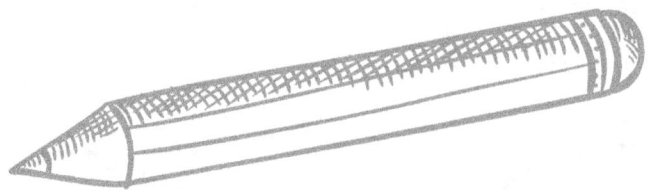

HOW TO DRAW SNAIL

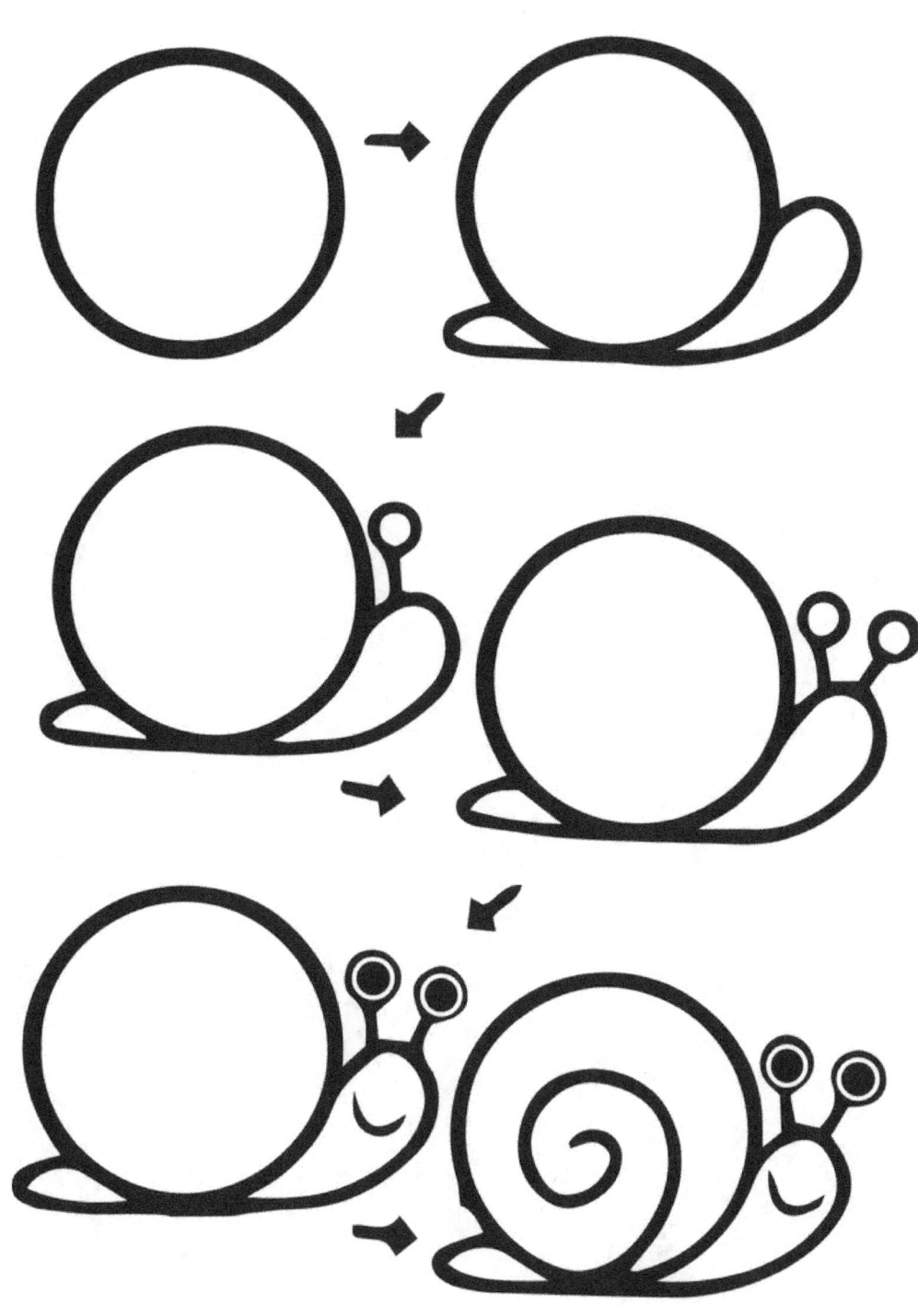

Redraw the previous animal

HOW TO DRAW RABBIT

Redraw the previous animal

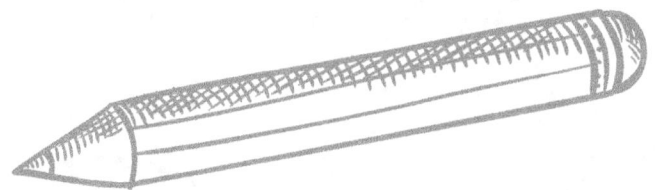

HOW TO DRAW ROOSTER

Redraw the previous animal

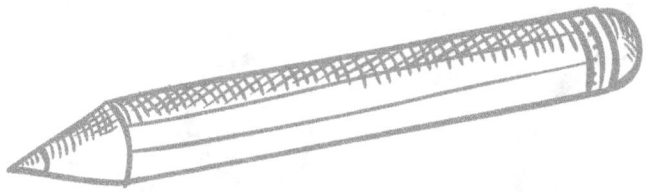

HOW TO DRAW OWL

Redraw the previous animal

HOW TO DRAW PANDA

Redraw the previous animal

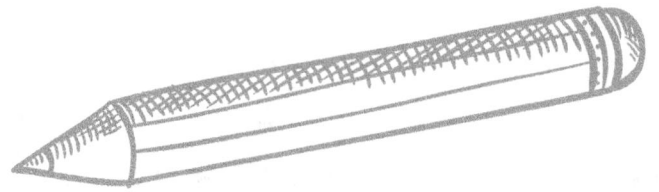

HOW TO DRAW OWL

Redraw the previous animal

HOW TO DRAW LADYBUG

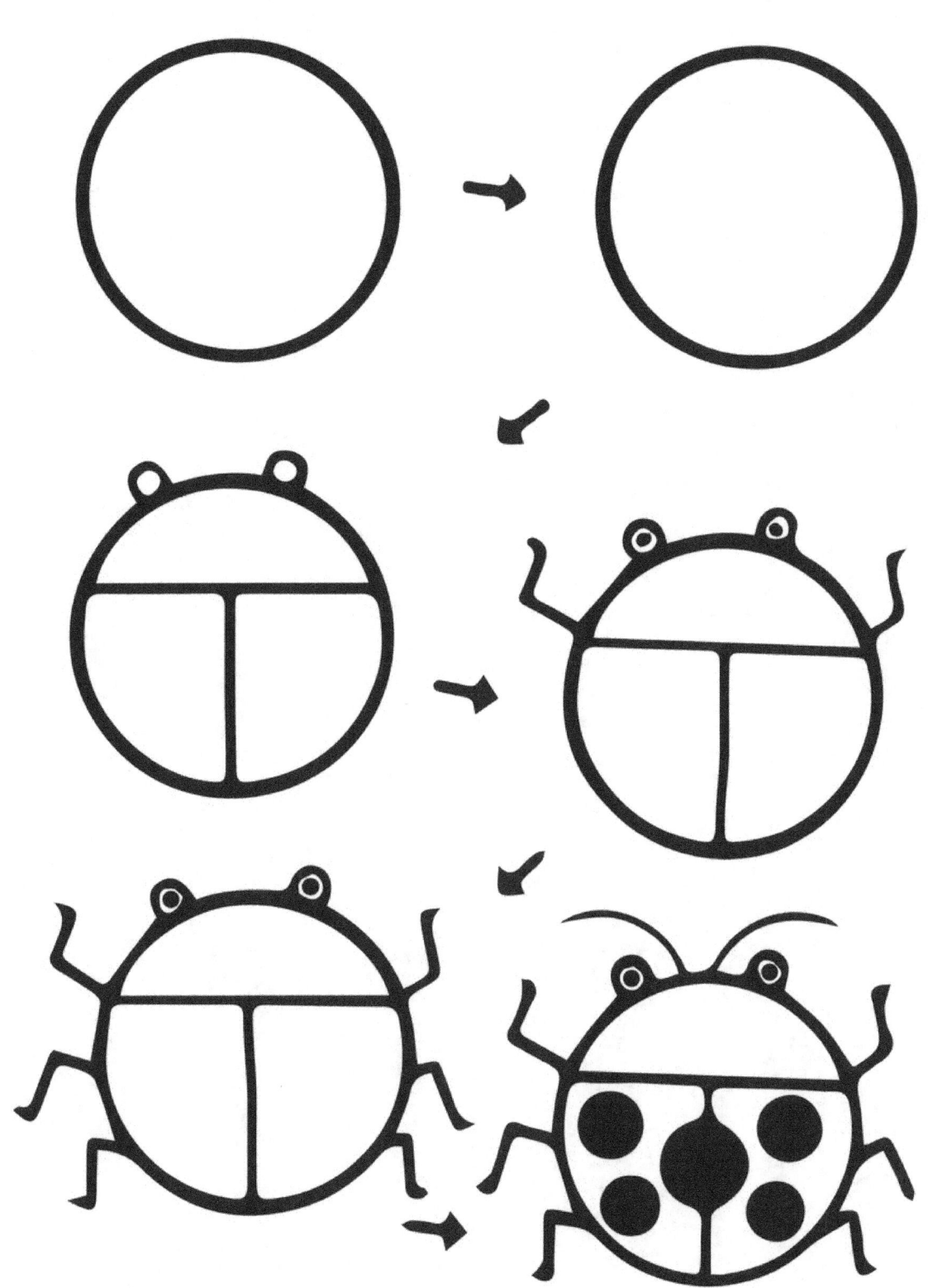

Redraw the previous animal

HOW TO DRAW MONKEY

Redraw the previous animal

HOW TO DRAW GOLDFISH

Redraw the previous animal

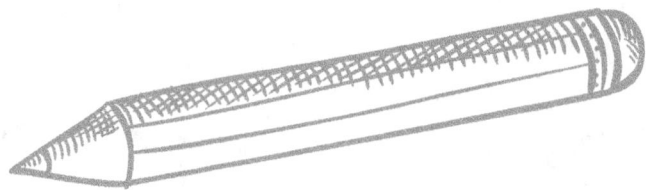

HOW TO DRAW HEN

Redraw the previous animal

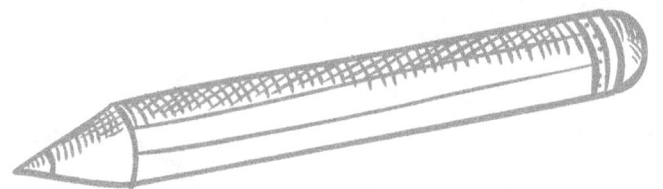

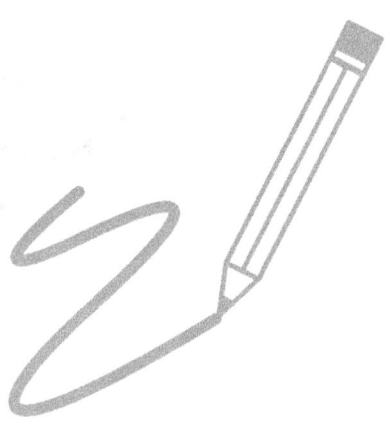

HOW TO DRAW EAGLE

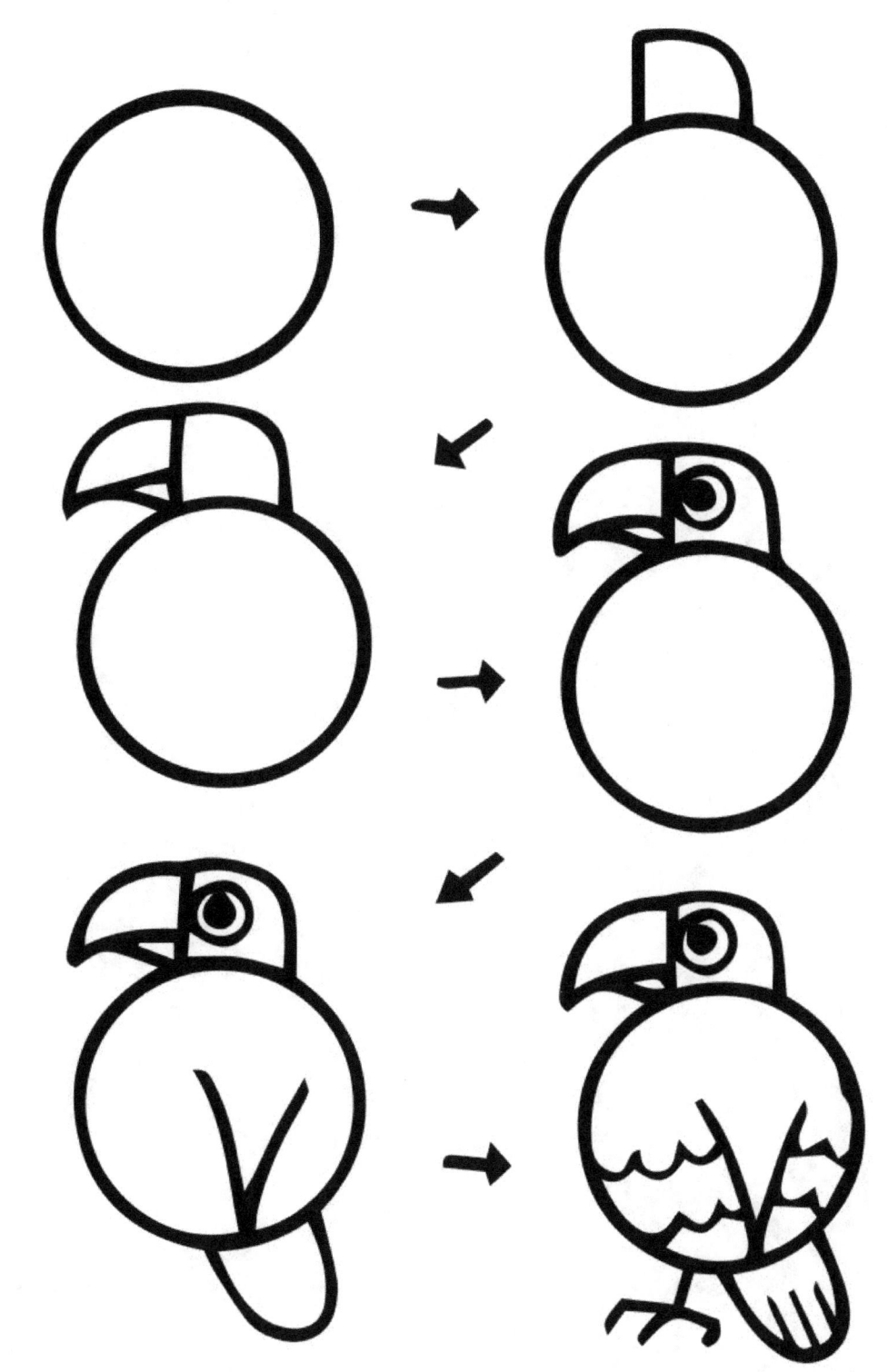

Redraw the previous animal

HOW TO DRAW FISH

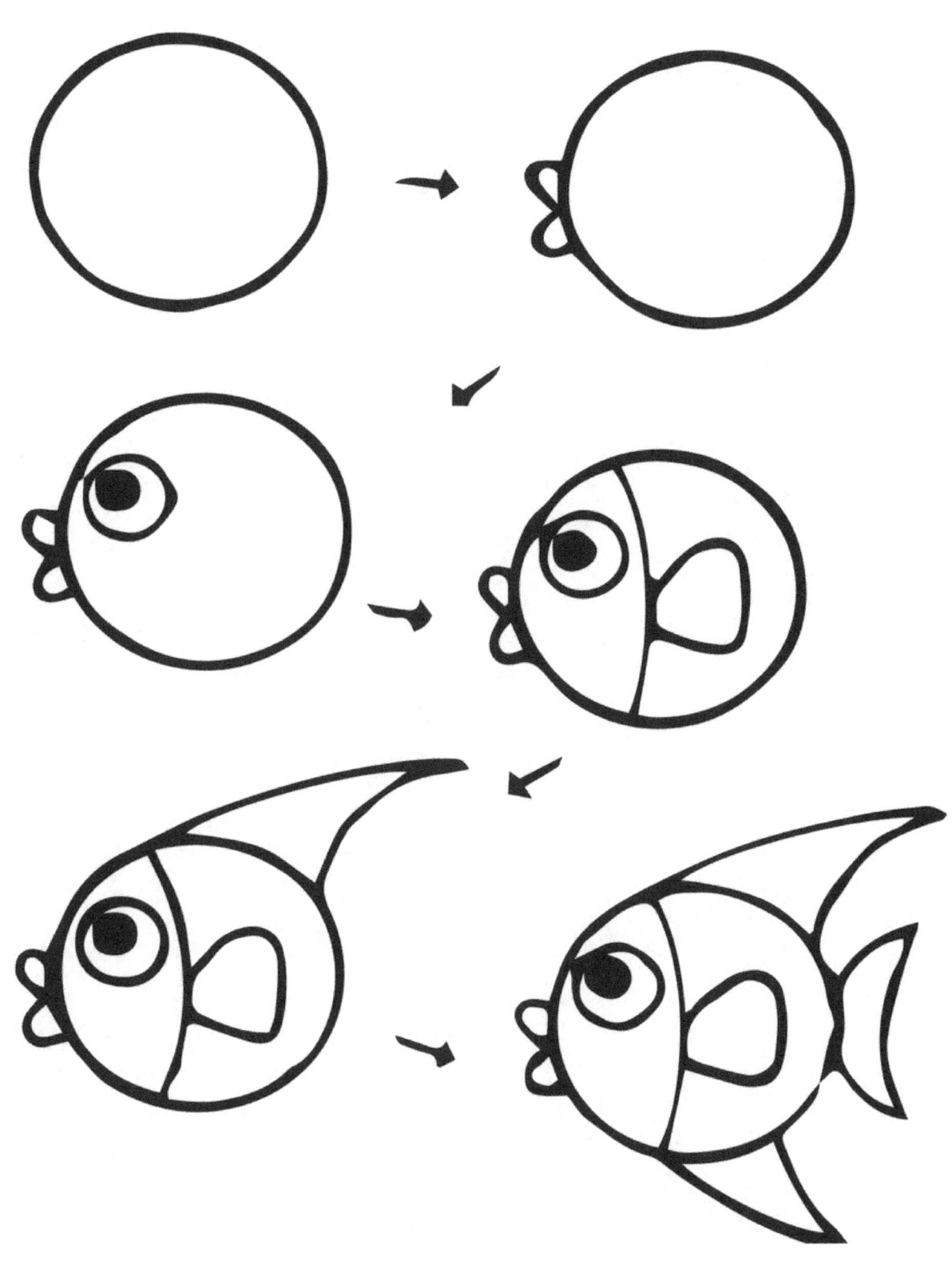

Redraw the previous animal

HOW TO DRAW CRAB

Redraw the previous animal

HOW TO DRAW DOG

Redraw the previous animal

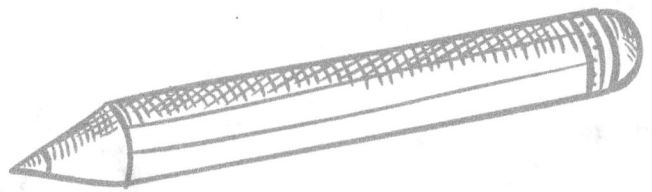

HOW TO DRAW CAT

Redraw the previous animal

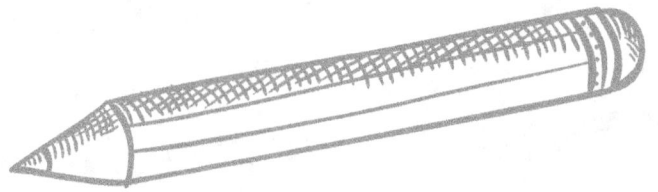

HOW TO DRAW CHICKEN

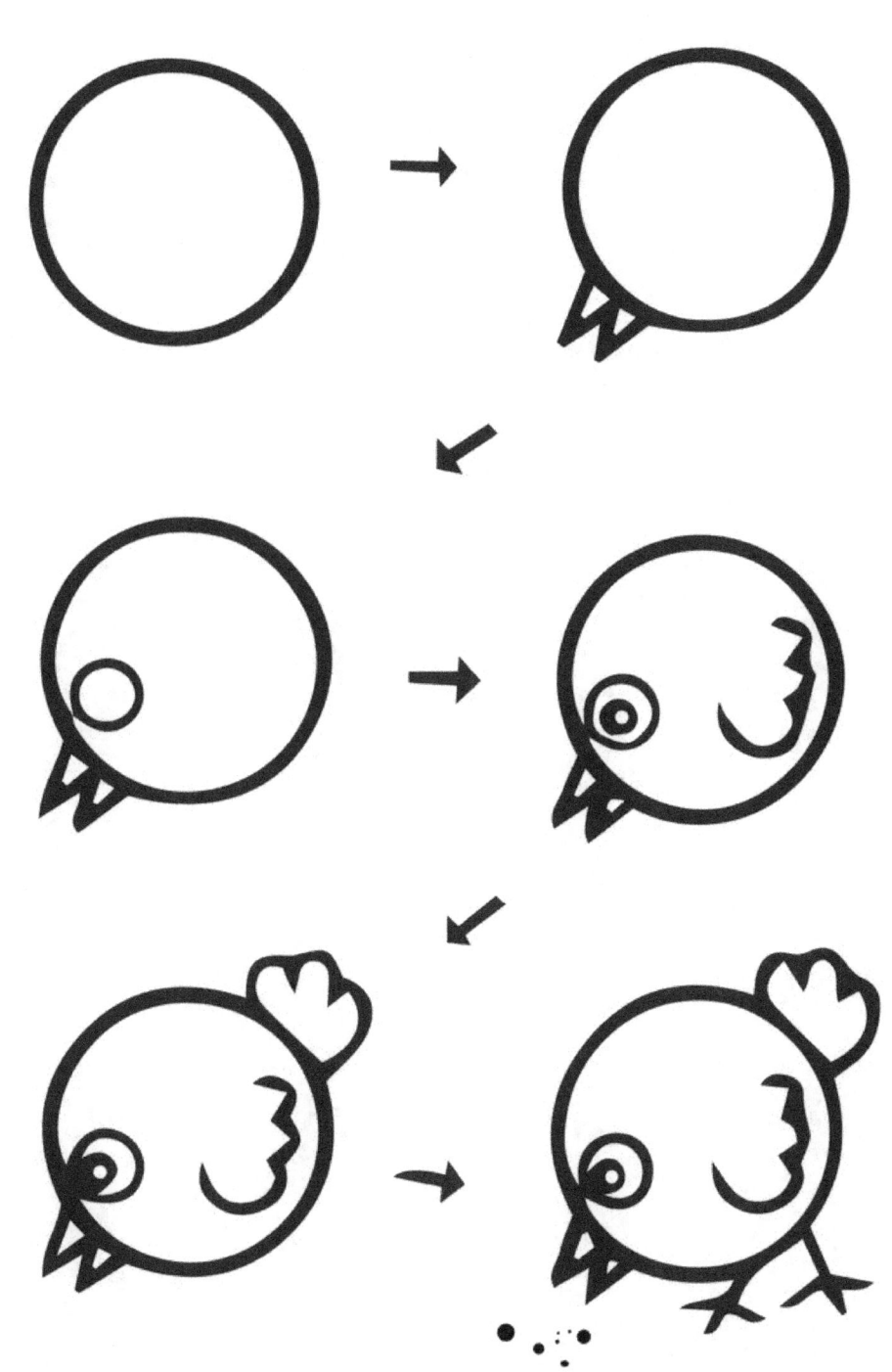

Redraw the previous animal

HOW TO DRAW BULL

Redraw the previous animal

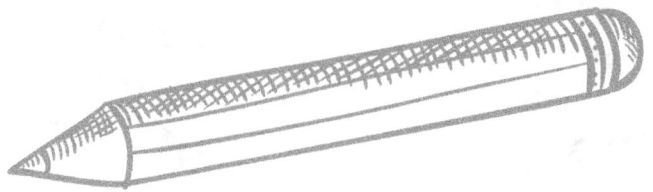

HOW TO DRAW BEAR

Redraw the previous animal

HOW TO DRAW TURKEY

Redraw the previous animal

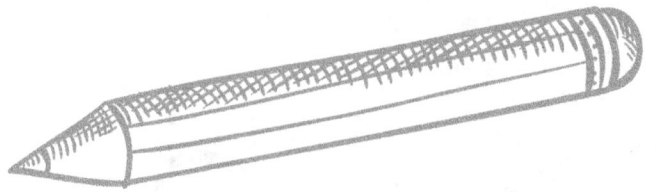

HOW TO DRAW TURTLE

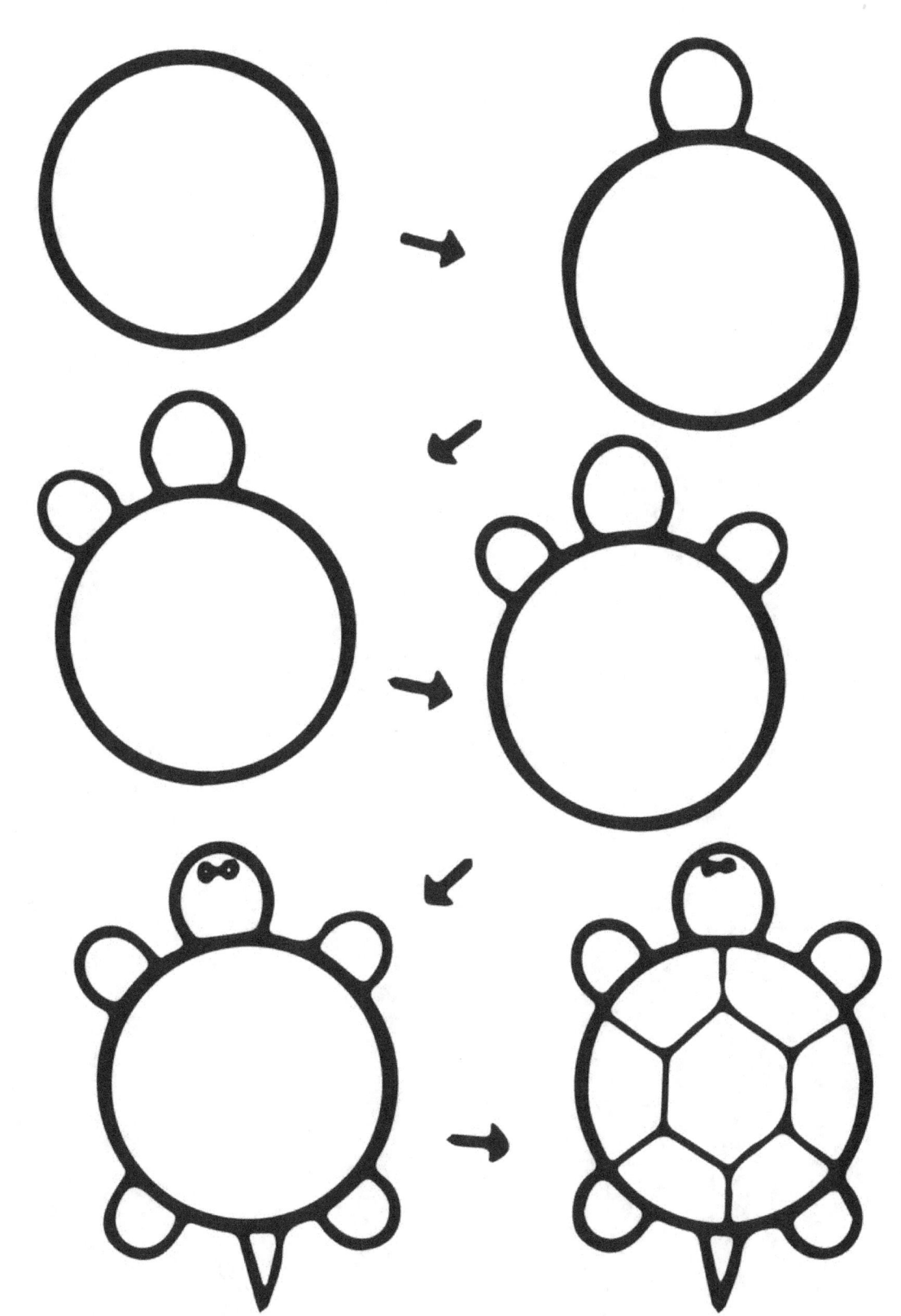

Redraw the previous animal

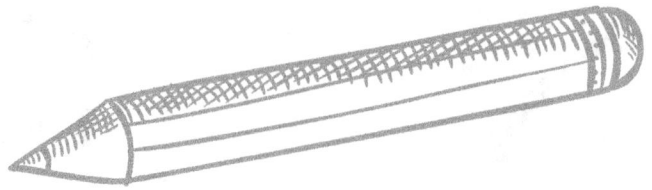

HOW TO DRAW

STEP 1

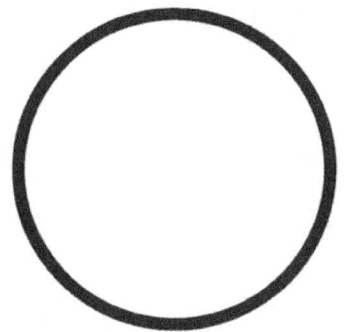

STEP 2

STEP 3

STEP 4

STEP 5

STEP 6

Redraw the previous animal

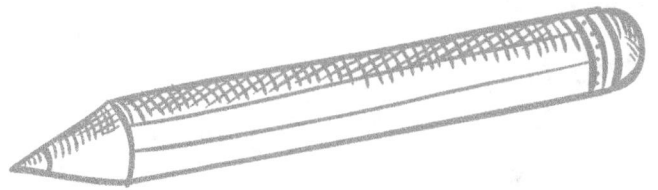

HOW TO DRAW

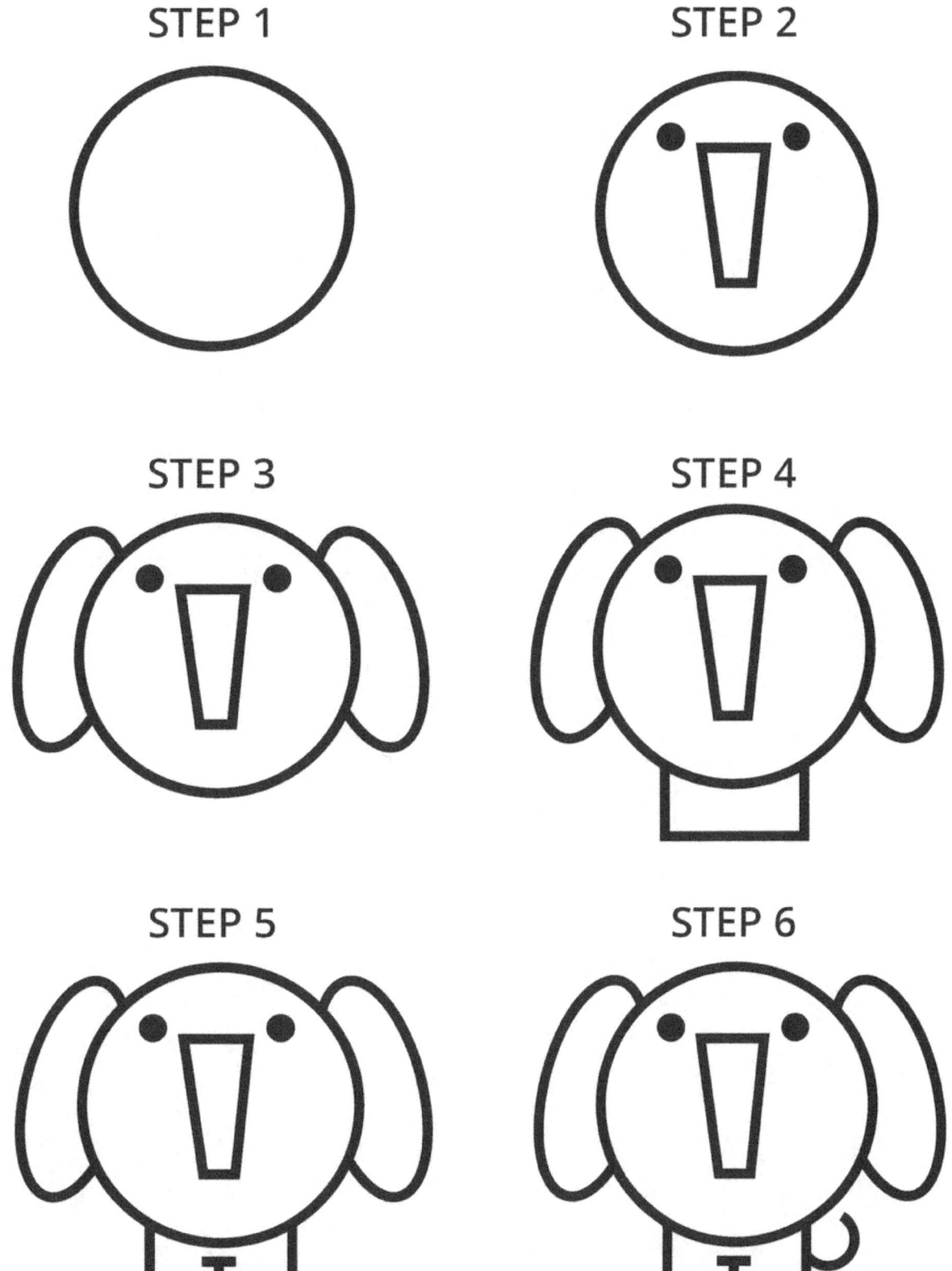

Redraw the previous animal

HOW TO DRAW

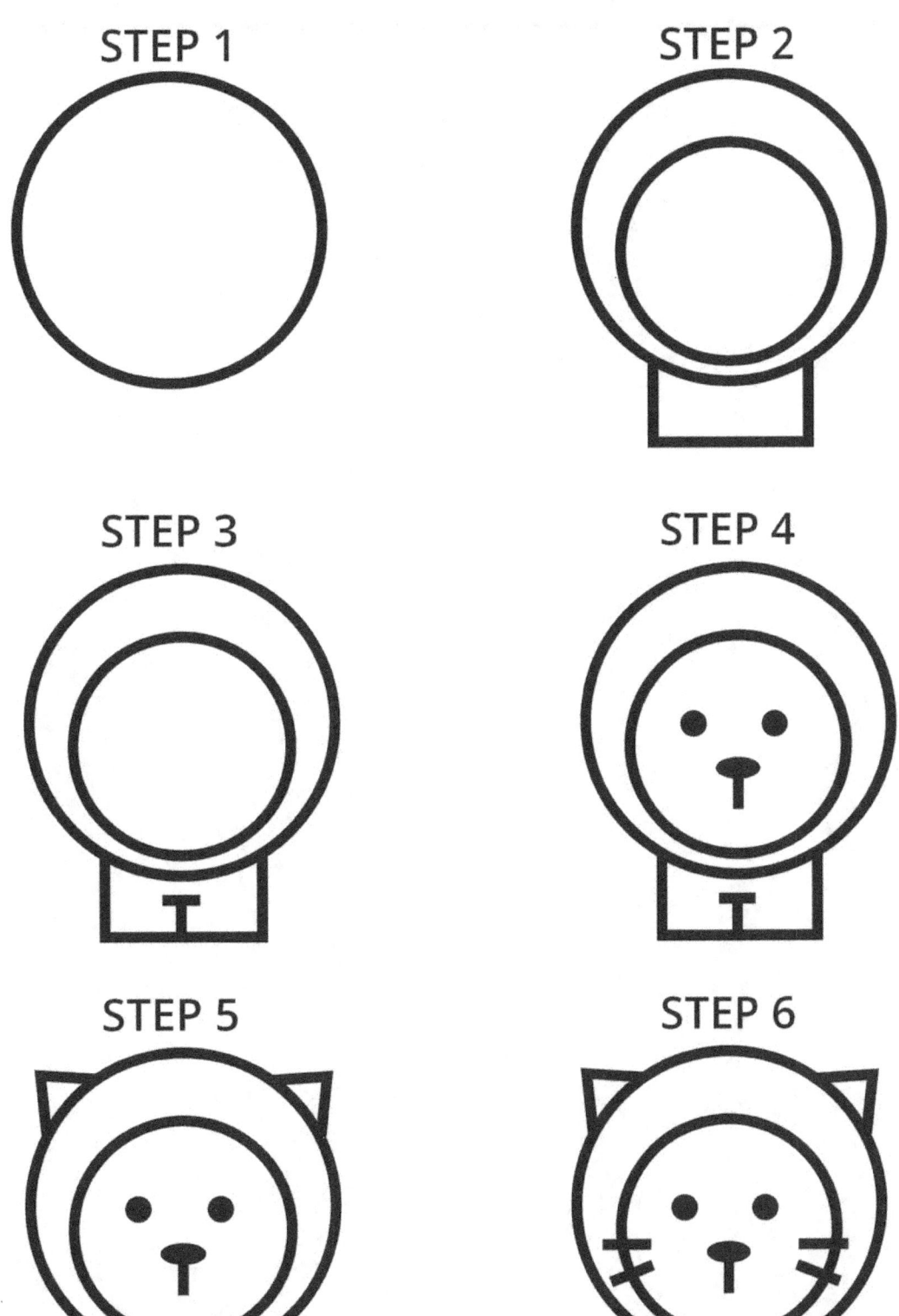

Redraw the previous animal

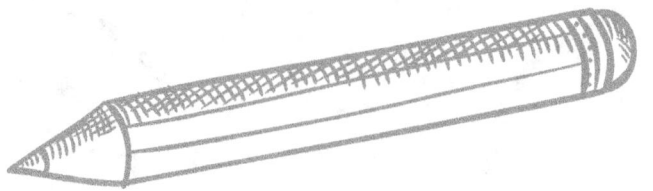

HOW TO DRAW

STEP 1

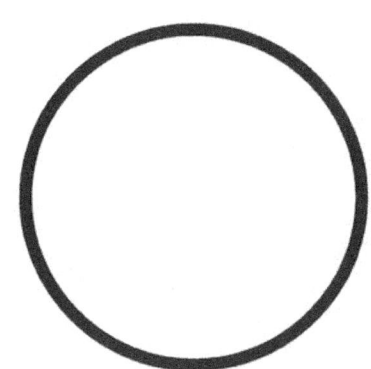

STEP 2

STEP 3

STEP 4

STEP 5

STEP 6

Redraw the previous animal

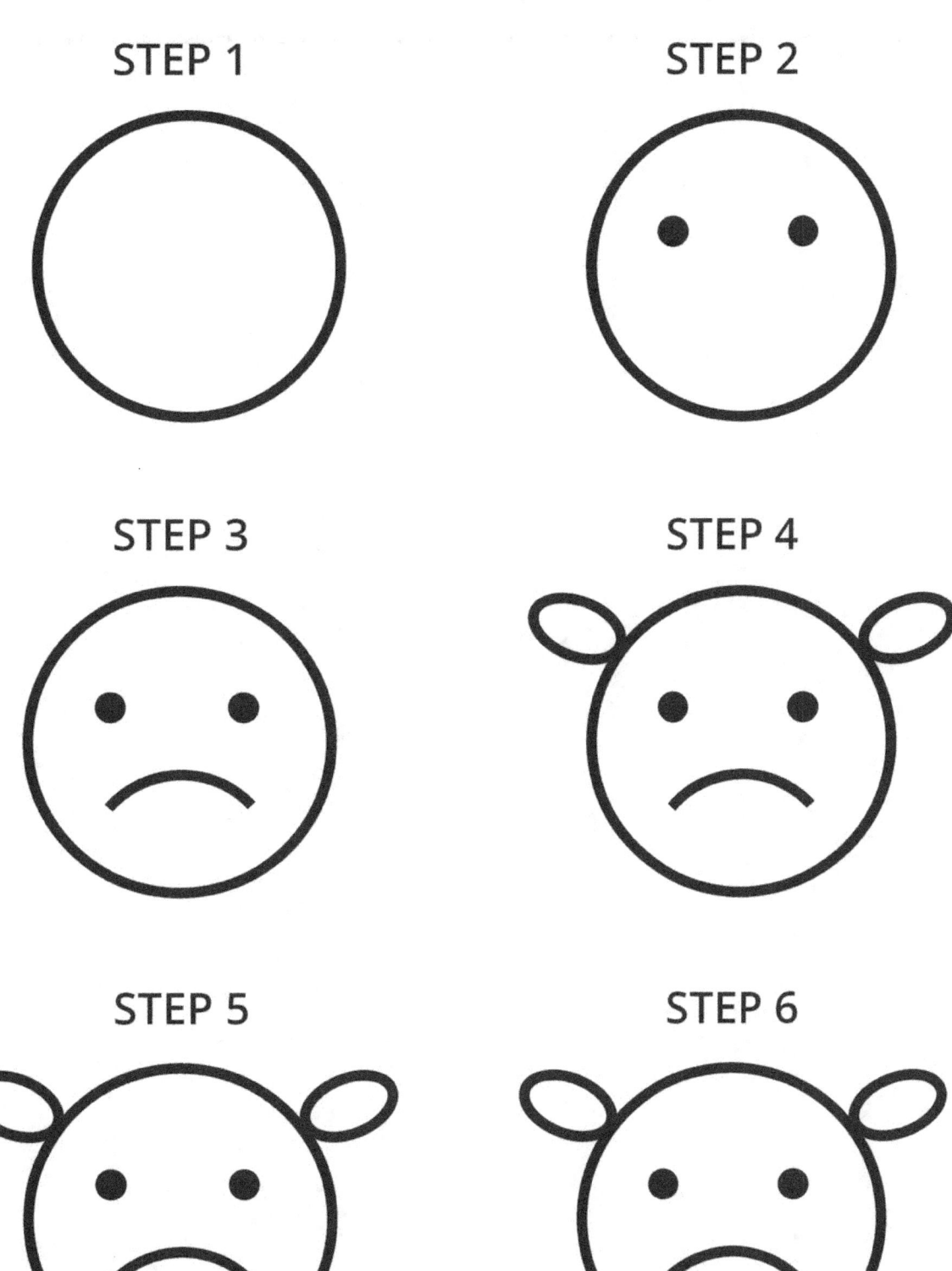

Redraw the previous animal

HOW TO DRAW

STEP 1

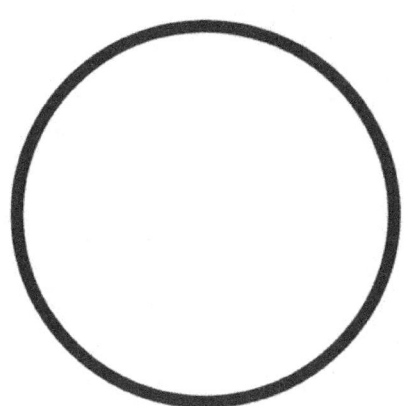

STEP 2

STEP 3

STEP 4

STEP 5

STEP 6

Redraw the previous animal

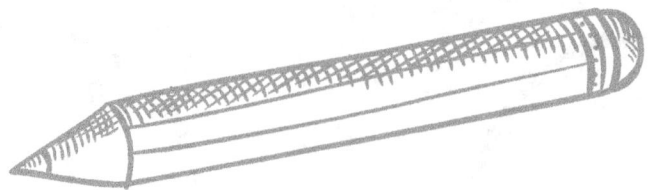

HOW TO DRAW

STEP 1　　STEP 2

STEP 3　　STEP 4

STEP 5　　STEP 6

Redraw the previous animal

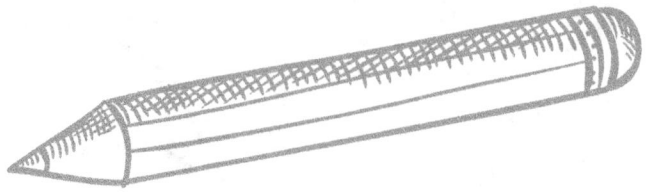

HOW TO DRAW

Redraw the previous animal

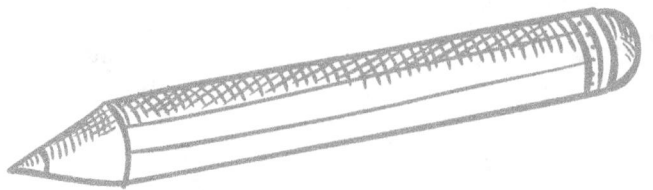

HOW TO DRAW

STEP 1
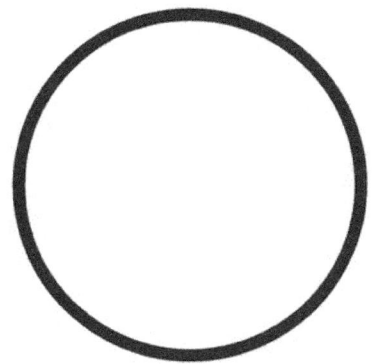

STEP 2
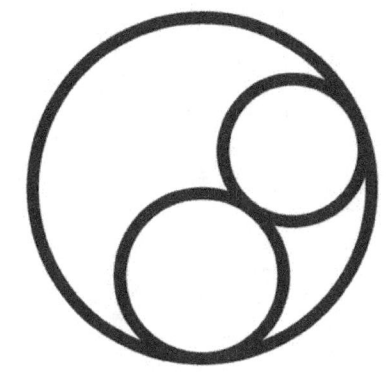

STEP 3

STEP 4

STEP 5

STEP 6

Redraw the previous animal

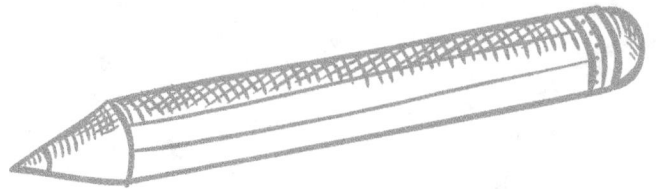

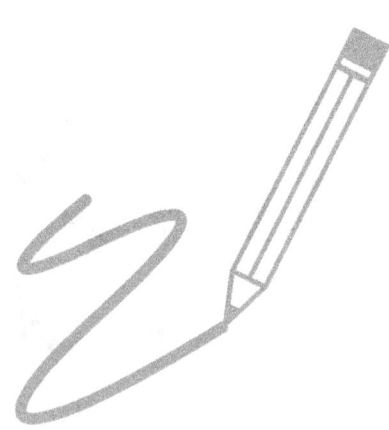

HOW TO DRAW

STEP 1

STEP 2

STEP 3

STEP 4

STEP 5

STEP 6

Redraw the previous animal

HOW TO DRAW

STEP 1
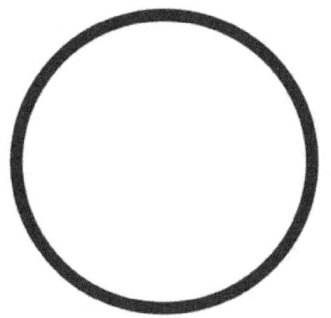

STEP 2
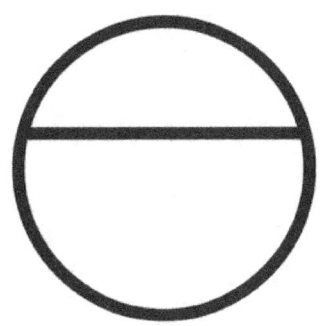

STEP 3
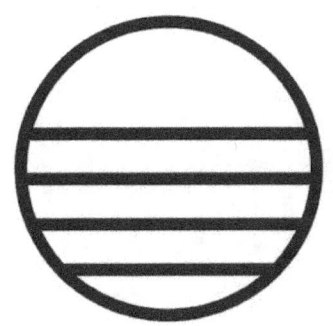

STEP 4

STEP 5

STEP 6

Redraw the previous animal

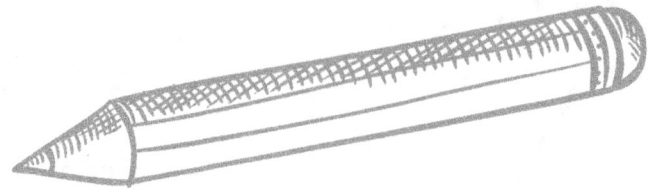

HOW TO DRAW

STEP 1

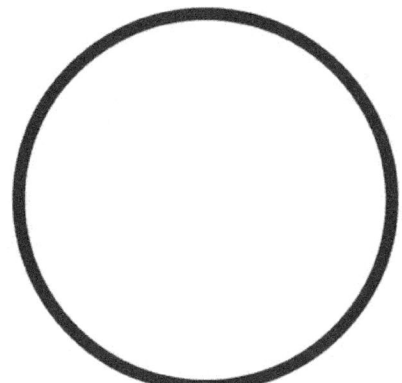

STEP 2

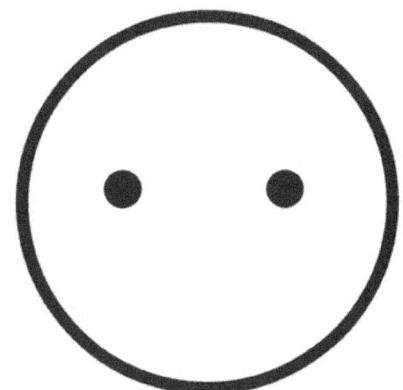

STEP 3

STEP 4

STEP 5

STEP 6

Redraw the previous animal

HOW TO DRAW

STEP 1

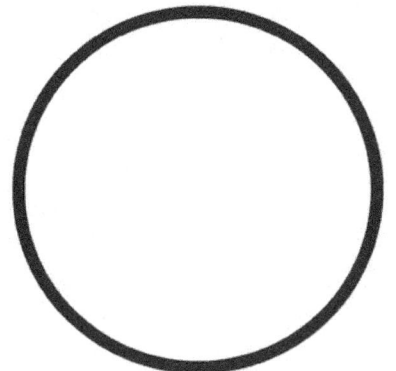

STEP 2

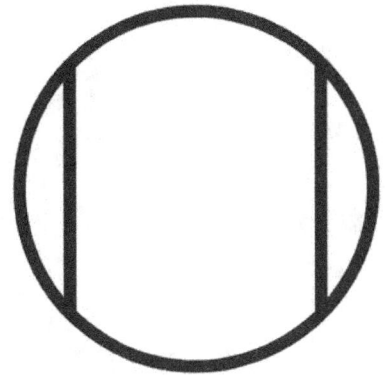

STEP 3

STEP 4

STEP 5

STEP 6

Redraw the previous animal

HOW TO DRAW

STEP 1

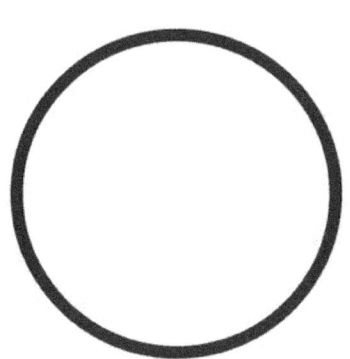

STEP 2

STEP 3

STEP 4

STEP 5

STEP 6

Redraw the previous animal

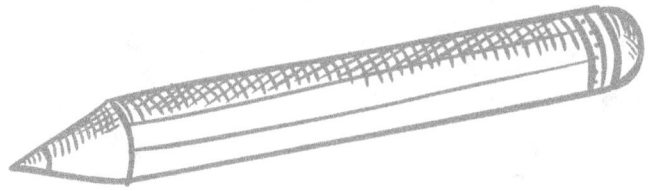

HOW TO DRAW

STEP 1
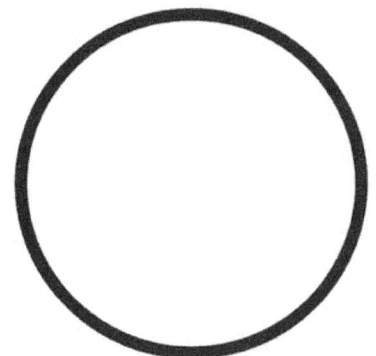

STEP 2

STEP 3

STEP 4

STEP 5

STEP 6
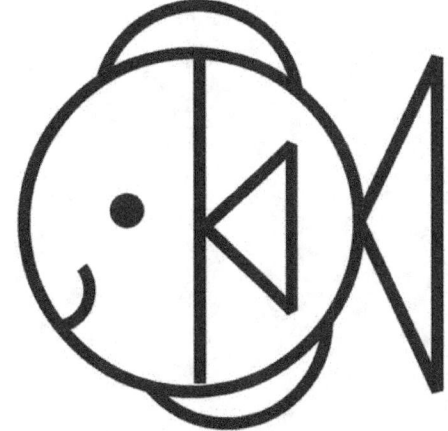

Redraw the previous animal

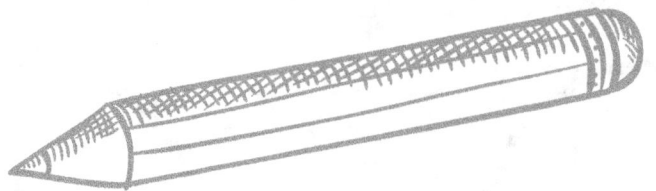

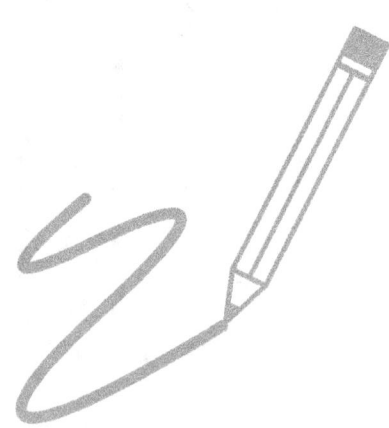

HOW TO DRAW

STEP 1

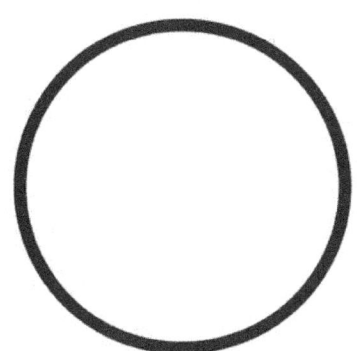

STEP 2

STEP 3

STEP 4

STEP 5

STEP 6

Redraw the previous animal

Redraw the previous animal

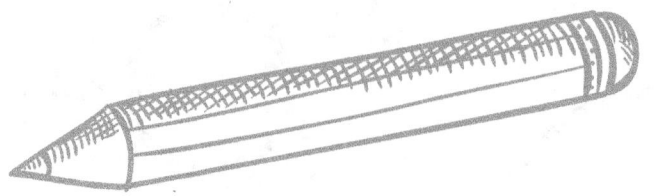

HOW TO DRAW

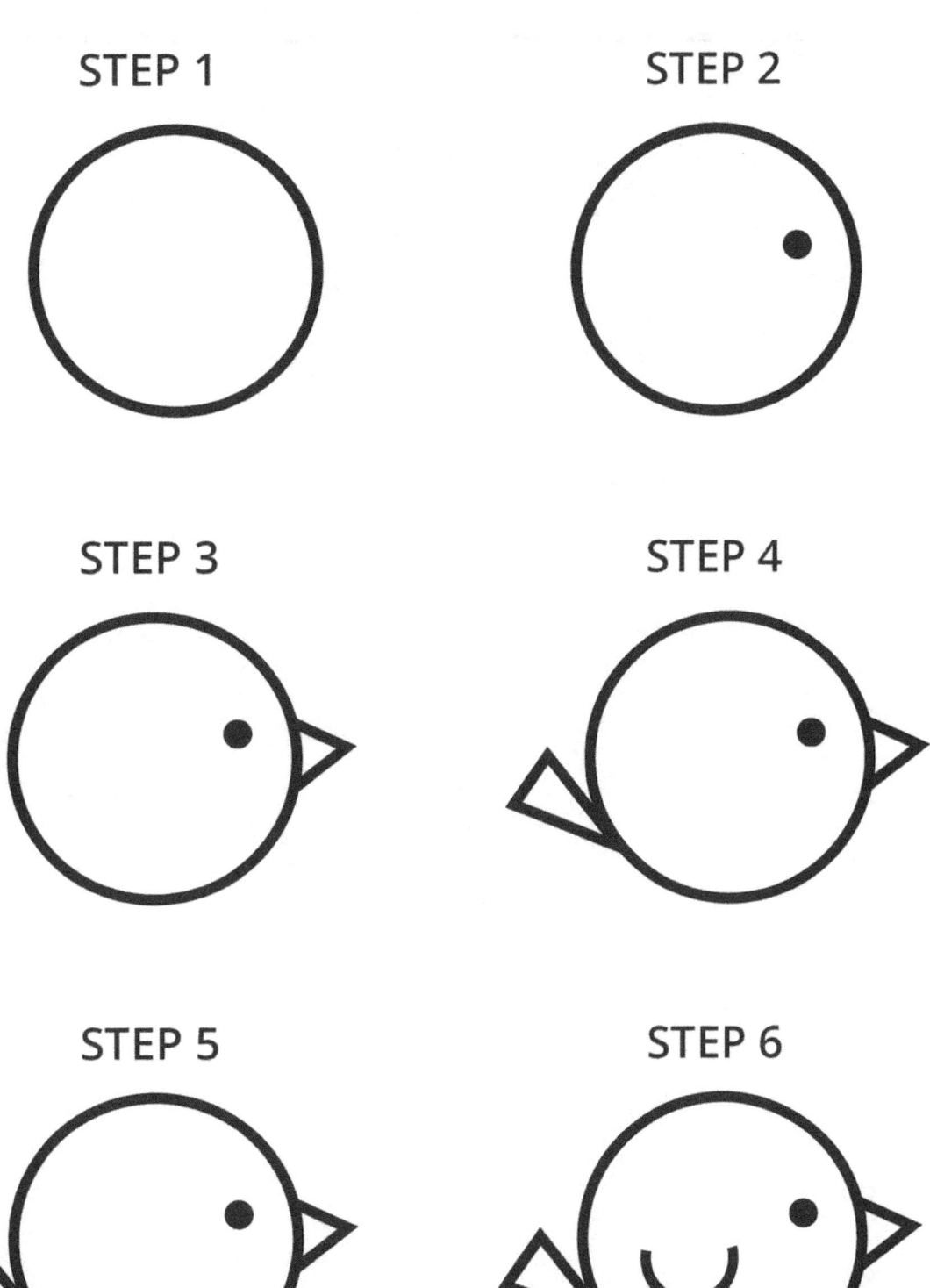

Redraw the previous animal

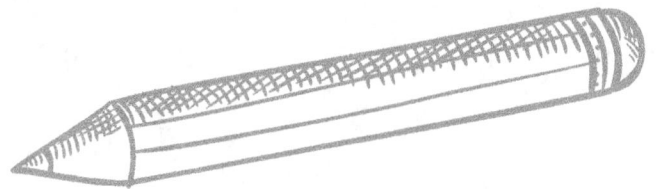

HOW TO DRAW

STEP 1

STEP 2

STEP 3

STEP 4

STEP 5

STEP 6

Redraw the previous animal

HOW TO DRAW

Redraw the previous animal

Redraw the previous animal

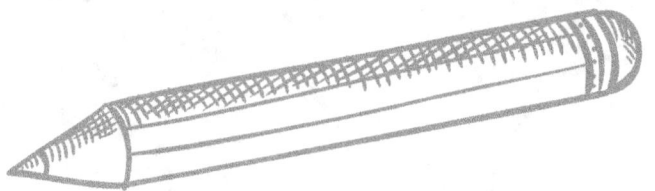

HOW TO DRAW

Redraw the previous animal

HOW TO DRAW

STEP 1
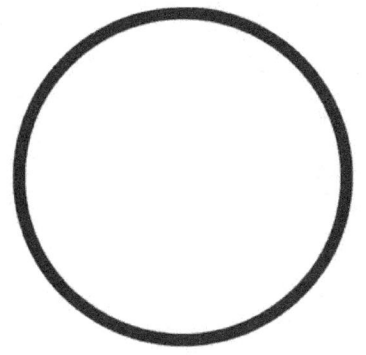

STEP 2

STEP 3

STEP 4

STEP 5

STEP 6

Redraw the previous animal

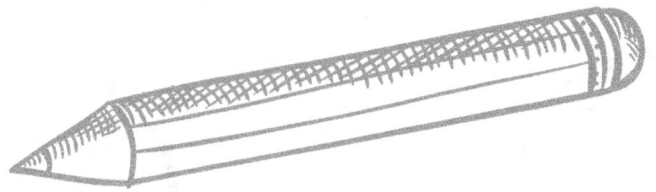

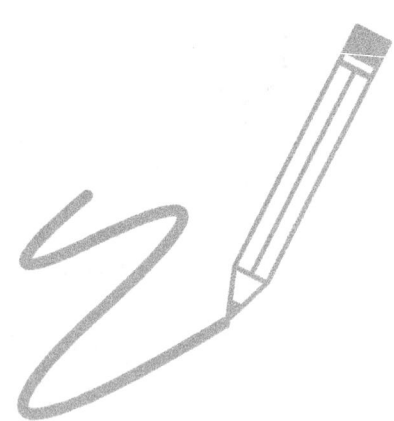

HOW TO DRAW

STEP 1
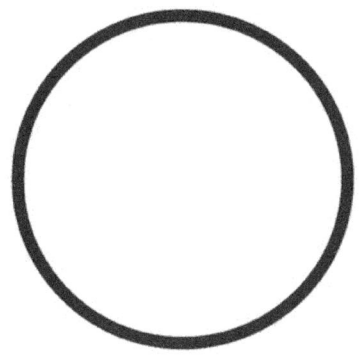

STEP 2

STEP 3

STEP 4

STEP 5

STEP 6

Redraw the previous animal

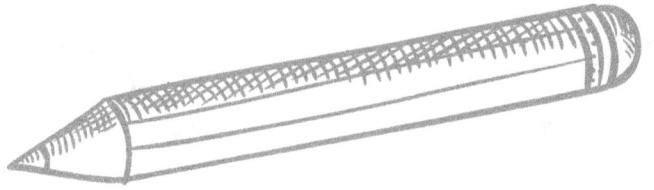

HOW TO DRAW

STEP 1

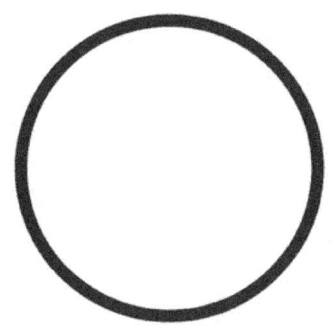

STEP 2

STEP 3

STEP 4

STEP 5

STEP 6

Redraw the previous animal

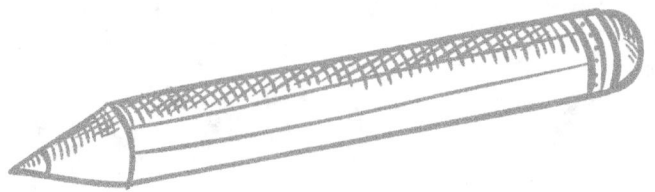

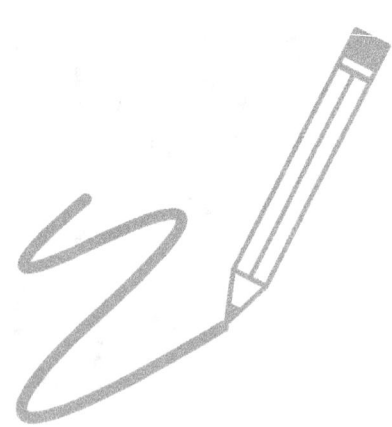

HOW TO DRAW

STEP 1

STEP 2

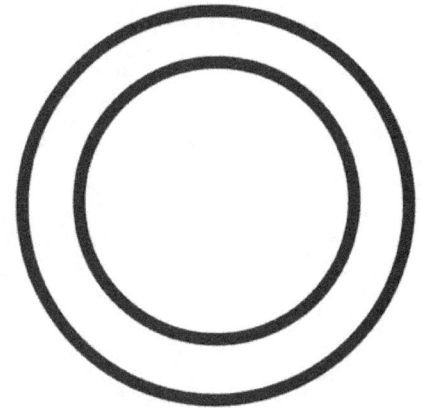

STEP 3

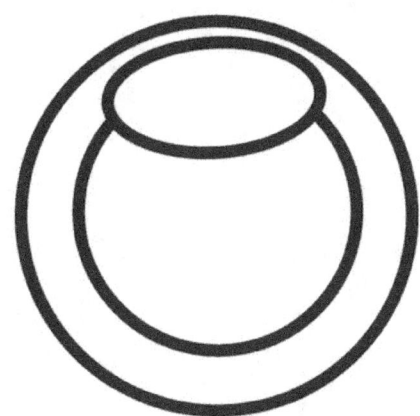

STEP 4

STEP 5

STEP 6

Redraw the previous animal

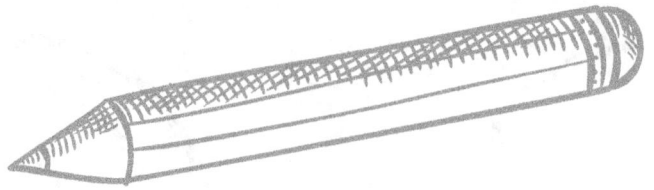

HOW TO DRAW

STEP 1

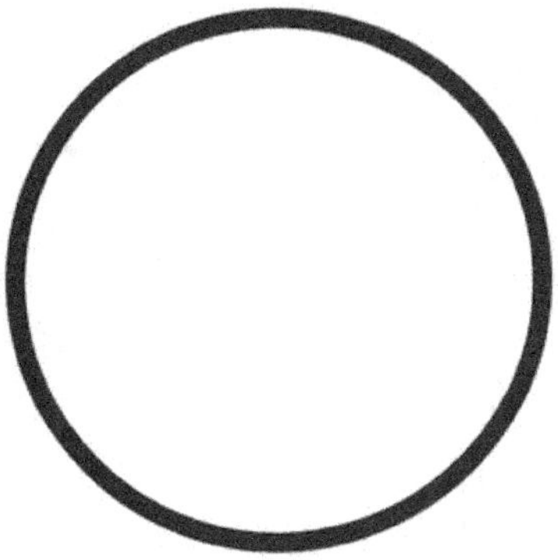

STEP 2

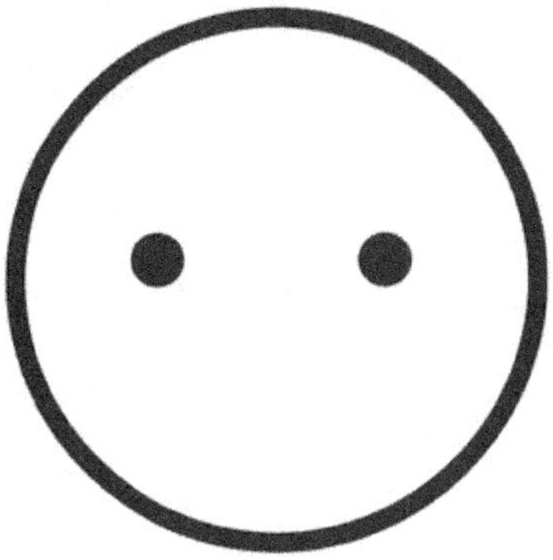

STEP 3

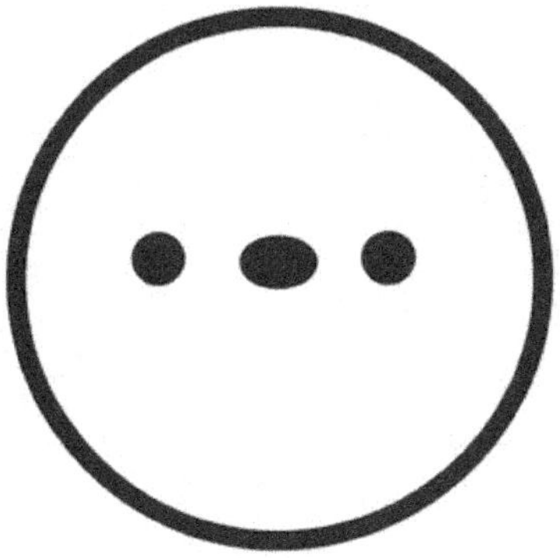

STEP 4

STEP 5

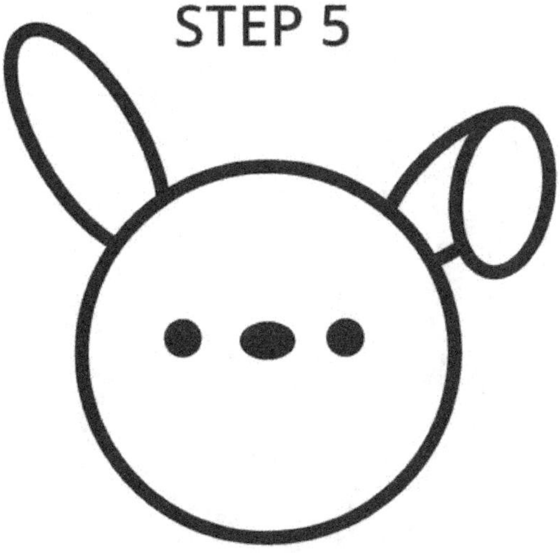

STEP 6

Redraw the previous animal

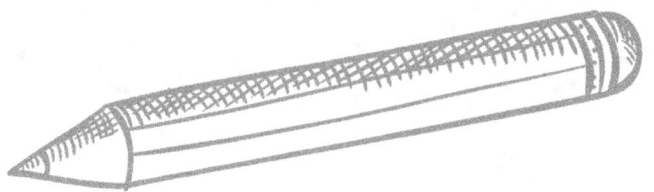

HOW TO DRAW

STEP 1

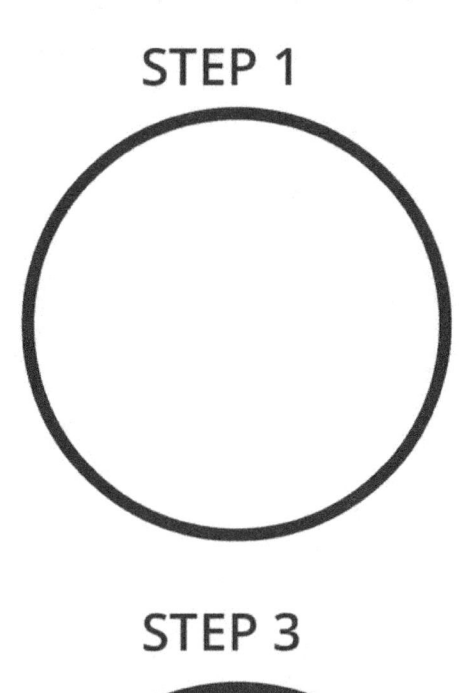

STEP 2

STEP 3

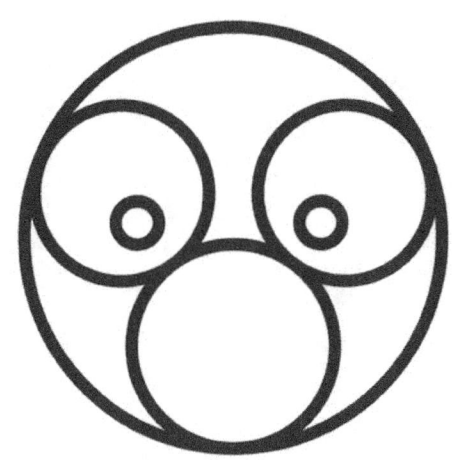

STEP 4

STEP 5

STEP 6

Redraw the previous animal

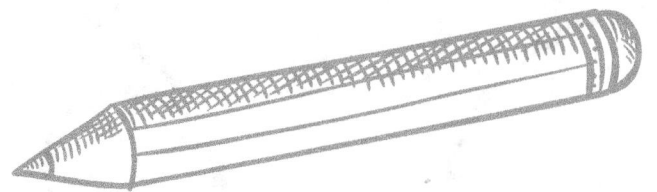

HOW TO DRAW

STEP 1

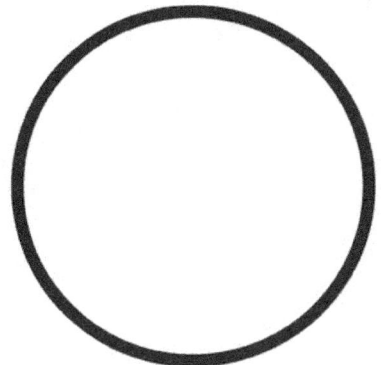

STEP 2

STEP 3

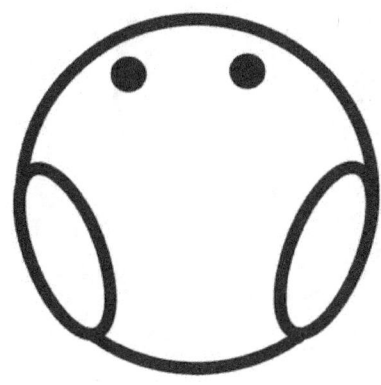

STEP 4

STEP 5

STEP 6

Redraw the previous animal

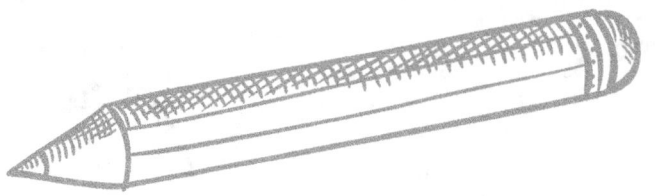

HOW TO DRAW

STEP 1

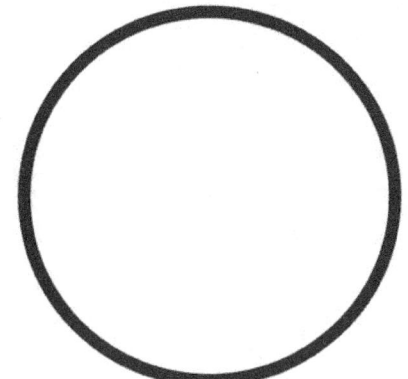

STEP 2

STEP 3

STEP 4

STEP 5

STEP 6

Redraw the previous animal

How to draw animals step by step

BONUS

How to draw cat

How to draw cat

Redraw the previous animal

How to draw a Dinosaure

How to draw a Dinosaure

How to draw a Dinosaure

How to draw a Dinosaure

Redraw the previous animal

Thank you!

We hope you enjoyed our book

As a small family company, your feedback is very important to us.

Please let us know how you like our book at:

 ICONICBOOKS.JOURNEY@GMAIL.COM

 /ICONICBOOKS.JOURNEY

 /ICONICBOOKS.JOURNEY

SCAN ME

www.ingramcontent.com/pod-product-compliance
Lightning Source LLC
LaVergne TN
LVHW060202080526
838202LV00052B/4185